The SHEPHERD'S GIFT

The First Christmas Mourning

JOHN RATERMAN

ISBN 978-1-64300-564-5 (Paperback)
ISBN 978-1-64300-565-2 (Digital)

Covenant Books, Inc.
11661 Hwy 707
Murrells Inlet, SC 29576
www.covenantbooks.com

DEDICATION

To my beautiful wife Mary, the mother of my seven children. You were always there, through my grieving and anger, even when I wasn't there for the rest of the family. To Michael, Lisa and Cathy, my three children in heaven. May the Lord hold you close until we meet again.

CHAPTER 1

The night was cold, and the wind blew at his back as he tended the sheep he had watched since he was a young boy. Jonas used to love to spend the night up on this hill, enjoying the peaceful sounds of his contented herd. The dog circled the flock slowly, careful not to spook the sheep but ensuring that none of the lambs wandered away into the night and the craggy hills that took several of them every year. Jonas hardly noticed the activities of the dog who knew his master was not able to relax, leading a restless life devoid of the peace he once knew. That peace was lost when he lost his daughter three years ago.

Although it was not much of a town but more like a village, Jonas and his family had lived here all of his life. His father, who passed more than a decade ago, was a shepherd, and his father's father was a shepherd right here on this hill. The hill was nothing special, but all the other shepherds knew this as Jonas's hill and respected the exclusive grazing rights that were historically respected in this area. The hill was rich in grass for the hundred or so sheep he had accumulated since last spring, and many of the ewes were expected to birth several dozen more within the next three months. Nothing had changed much since he was a small child, raising the sheep, shearing some for valuable wool, and driving many of them to market in Jerusalem for use in the religious sacrifices and rituals in the Temple.

Jonas liked going to Jerusalem, even though the Roman mercenaries occupied the capital city with a tight fist and a condescending attitude. He could not even *mention* Jerusalem without his youngest, five-year-old Sarah, beginning to pack and telling everyone all the things she planned to do and see while she was there. While her older sisters liked to spend time in the home with their mother, spinning wool into yarn and preparing meals, Sarah preferred the open air of the hill, playing up there with the lambs and their dog, Caesar. It was Caesar's job to herd the flock and prevent stragglers from wandering away where jackals and other dangers awaited them. Sarah, however, saw Caesar's role as a loyal playmate and constant companion, often in direct conflict with her father's wishes and requirements.

Ezekiel was the eldest son of Jonas and his wife, Esther, and now at the age of fifteen, he had completed his Hebrew studies and was preparing for his eventual role as the lead shepherd of the family flock. This would be years from now as Jonas was still a healthy man of thirty-seven, although the years on that hill had left his face ruddy and rough, darkened since youth by the sunny climate of Judea. As a devout Jew, Jonas kept his head covered as instructed by the law but secretly appreciated the cover it provided for his rapidly balding head. Always respectful of his father, Ezekiel smirked at his father's vanity and prayed, probably in vain, that his currently thick crop of hair would be spared this common fate.

Sarah's older sisters, Beth and Naomi, were ten and twelve years old, respectively, and found working with the sheep to be dirty, smelly jobs that they preferred to avoid whenever possible. They would make themselves available to their mother at every call so as to avoid the more labor-intensive work in the spring of shearing and castrations, especially the castrations. Their nimble hands were quite adept at spinning the bleached wool into fine yarns that could be sold at the marketplace or used to make their new tunics every spring. At just twelve years old, Naomi was one of the best spinners of wool yarn in their town, and other shepherds often brought bleached wool to her to earn a few dinars for her own use. Several young men of the town expressed interest in marriage to Naomi in three or four years, and Jonas began wondering how much of a dowry would be required of him. Though two years younger, Beth used her age for sympathy during each negotiation in the marketplace to gain a slight premium to the established prices for spun yarn.

Esther was the head-of-household whether Jonas acknowledged this reality or not. She gave the four children their chores and made sure they were completed promptly and thoroughly. She also made a trip to the well every morning to collect the day's water for drinking and cooking with a large water jug. As it was several hundred yards to the well, many of the women of the town would "rest" when they arrived, spending those precious minutes every morning talking to the other women, well out of the view of their husbands. Even young Sarah had responsibilities for preparing the rough wooden table for dinner and for hauling enough water from the nearby community well to wash hands and dishes as dictated by Jewish law. Sarah just could not understand why she had to make two trips one day per week as she was forbidden to haul water on the Sabbath, but she completed her task quickly in case she had the opportunity to accompany her daddy onto the hill for the night, the task she truly loved.

Although they were poor, his family had enjoyed their life together, raising their herd, keeping their small home clean and warm, sharing meals whenever his work allowed, and going to the Temple on the Sabbath to thank God for the gifts they had received and pay homage to the Lord as dictated by the Law.

Esther had also named their dog more than five years ago. In spite of Jonas's strong objections, Esther insisted that this demanding little puppy be named after the Emperor of Rome, as his empire had conquered Judea as it had conquered most of the world at that time. Caesar demanded their attention, complained loudly when things went awry, and consumed too much of the meager foodstuffs they could hardly spare. Just like the emperor! Every spring, as they took the flock to market, the emperor's tax thugs would demand payment, often extorting more than the emperor required so as to secure their own comfort. Their friends had blanched when told of the puppy's name as every man and woman in this town despised the emperor and his Assyrian mercenaries that occupied the land promised to Moses by the Lord and recaptured by the great King David. When she told them *why* they gave the dog this name, they all laughed and made remarks about the similarity of the emperor and this mongrel puppy. They were the only Jewish family in all of Palestine that welcomed Caesar into their home!

But all that changed when Sarah died three years ago. Now, the rare times he visited the Temple on holy days, he spent less time praising his Lord and more time angrily wondering why his God had taken the joy from his life.

CHAPTER 2

That fateful night, Sarah packed dinner for her and her daddy and a little treat for Caesar who knew that when Sarah was up on the hill, he would enjoy playtime and snacks. Their dinner usually consisted of coarse barley bread, some dates, some figs, and some dried mutton. Esther would make sure she remembered her flute and her sheepskin blanket, as well as clothes warm enough to ensure her comfort. Jonas carried some kindling up the hill to build a small fire as this night was colder than usual.

Just a year earlier, Jonas would have to hold Sarah's hand to help her up the steep, rocky part of the hill, but now he struggles to keep up with her as she scampers over the difficult parts. There was a broader path on the other side of the hill that wound down to the main road to Jerusalem, but that was too far to walk. Jonas only used that path when he drove a large number of the lambs and castrated rams known as wethers to market. This late autumn time of year was tricky for Jonas as the rams and sheep were breeding in the fields and Sarah was a little too young to understand. Besides, that was her mother's job to explain as he had done so for Ezekiel. Jonas just had to keep Sarah away from the rams during this season as they could be quite aggressive. If Jonas had one trait that everyone recognized, it was his coddling care for young Sarah.

When they reached the summit of the hill, Caesar was resting, and the flock was grazing lazily in the plush grass, browned by the fall frost but still in great supply to feed them for weeks. Caesar sprang to his feet and ran to Sarah as soon as he saw her, and she knelt in the grass to greet her dear friend. She teased him with a piece of yarn on a stick while Jonas built the campfire in the same spot that had welcomed them for the past two weeks. The top of this hill did not offer much protection from the brisk wind, so Jonas made sure Sarah was bundled against the weather. Like all children, however, her activity raised her body temperature, and Jonas tolerated her removal of one layer of her clothes. She then spent the next few minutes brushing Caesar's long coat and pulling the knots and burrs from his multicolored fur, accumulated over the past four days since her last night on the hill. While Jonas built and tended the fire, Sarah dug in her little garden of poppy flowers, trying in vain to resurrect the blooms that faded toward their winter slumber. She had planted the flowers from seeds she harvested from their home garden last spring in hopes that it would make the hill a little prettier. She had to train Caesar to keep the sheep out of her little patch on top of her daddy's hill.

After little more than an hour, Caesar had had enough play time and nestled close to Jonas and the small fire. Caesar's real motivation was the pack of food Jonas had begun to unpack, knowing that either Sarah had packed something for him or she would give him a bit of her mutton. Frankly, he was indifferent to the source of the food, just so he got some. Once the fire was burning, Ezekiel came over from tending the flock, gave his father a kiss, rubbed Caesar behind his ears, and hugged Sarah high on his chest before heading down the hill to protect the house and the women therein. Since his bar mitzvah, Ezekiel had stepped up to assume more responsibilities as one of the "men" of the house. He was a fine son, a hard worker, and a great guardian of his three younger sisters. Like all the teenage boys his age, however, he had begun to pay more attention to the girls in their town, attention that was deflected by the girls' fathers but still hurting the productivity Jonas had come to expect from his son. Jonas could not complain as his attention was diverted at that same age.

Jonas was famished by the time dinnertime came on the mountain. He hungrily consumed the mutton, a large piece of the brown bread and then relaxed munching on the sweet dates and figs. Sarah, on the other hand, had little appetite tonight, and Jonas assumed that the frolicking with Caesar had worn her out. She rested her head on Caesar's midsection unwrapped her pack and brought out the sheepskin, secured like a bedroll, and carefully untied the leather straps. Once unrolled, Sarah picked up the small wooden flute her daddy had made for her for her last birthday that was tucked safely within the roll. She didn't know what he had been doing for those past few weeks preceding her birthday as he smoothed the stick on a rock and used his well-worn knife to hollow the branch and carve holes on the long side of the branch. Only when she unwrapped it on her birthday did she realize he had made her a flute, the best present she had ever received! He had taught her the tunes to several of King David's Psalms, and in no time, she could play the flute proficiently. Her flute provided a secondary benefit as it calmed the sheep and encouraged them to nestle into the knee high grass.

After playing her limited repertoire, Sarah would place the flute back into the pack, ensuring it was protected from damage while she rubbed the sheepskin across her soft cheeks and secreted her thumb into her mouth. Jonas had tried to break her of this habit but gave up whenever he saw her nestled with Caesar, her eyes closing and a look of total contentment enveloping her angelic face.

In the morning, Sarah usually woke early, returned the flute to the sheepskin roll, and secured the roll with the leather straps. When Jonas awoke from his brief three-hour slumber just moments before the sunrise, he expected to see Sarah petting Caesar, waiting for her daddy to walk her down the hill to begin her household chores. This morning started differently, as Sarah was sound asleep on the cold ground, Caesar having woken and begun his rousting of the flock while leaving his friend asleep.

When he shook Sarah, his hand brushed her face, and he felt the fever. She lay there, not sleeping but unconscious from an illness that caught Jonas completely by surprise. He kicked dirt on the barely glowing embers, threw the pack over his shoulder, and scooped Sarah into his arms to begin the rushed descent back to the house and the care of her mother. While he wanted to run, he knew that this part of the hill was treacherous, especially with the thin layer of frost that had accumulated this chilly night, and he was not going to endanger his young daughter further. The fever was enough. As he descended, he alternated calling her name and praying to God to help her wake up. Tears welled in his eyes as he could not tell if either Sarah or God could hear his desperate pleas.

When Jonas finally reached the base of the hill, he passed his son who was climbing the hill to assume his shepherding duties for the day. "Go wake the physician and rush him to the house. Sarah has a fever, and I am not able to wake her!" The panic was evident in Jonas's voice, and this coming from a rock of a man that once drove a pack of jackals away from the flock with his staff and a few rocks. His voice shook when he finally reached the door of the house. Beth met him at the door, noticing he was home earlier than normal. When she saw Sarah lying limp in his arms, she shrieked and began to cry.

Jonas barked, "Where is your mother? I need her now!" It was more of a command than a question. Naomi had heard the fiery exchange and told Jonas that her mother was down at the well collecting the needed water for the day.

"Go get her. NOW!"

Naomi rushed from the house and ran as fast as she was able the distance to the well. Although it was cold this morning, Naomi failed to notice as the family crisis overcame any personal concerns for comfort. As she approached the gaggle of ladies filling their water jugs and sharing the gossip of the day, Esther spotted her and knew by her urgency that something had happened.

"What's wrong? Did something happen to Beth? To Ezekiel?" Esther was not panicked but sternly insistent that her daughter inform her of the situation.

By now, Naomi had caught her breath and began to cry. "Daddy came home carrying Sarah. He was not able to wake her this morning and says she has a bad fever." Esther toppled the water jug, not noticing or caring if it broke, running back to the house to take care of her baby. As an afterthought, she shouted back to Naomi to get the doctor to the house, neither of them realizing that Ezekiel had already reached him and was hurrying him back to their house.

When Esther arrived at the house, the town doctor was there already, using the little water left in the house to dampen the rags needed to cool Sarah's fever. The doctor opened his satchel and removed a small wineskin half-filled with a dark liquid that looked bad and smelled even worse. He moved the oil lamp close to her face and raised one of her eyelids, trying to determine what other effects the fever might have caused.

"Lift her head so we can try to get some of this elixir into her. If she ate something bad, she will likely vomit this, and if that is not the issue, this has some powers to break a fever," explained the doctor, speculating to himself that this illness was not of a routine nature and her fate might be out of his hands and already in the hands of God. Sarah coughed, still unconscious, as some of the fluid clearly went down her windpipe but soon stopped coughing and resumed her unchanging slumber.

By now, several of the ladies from the well had arrived at the house, carrying the now-filled water jar that Esther had abandoned when Naomi had given her the news. While Jonas did not say anything, he cynically wondered whether they really wanted to help or were collecting information for their next round of gossip. Jonas chastised himself, ashamed that his mind wandered to such ugly thoughts when his focus should be on prayer for his daughter.

Jonas went outside, the small home now too crowded with people wanting to help. Jonas needed to be alone with his God.

CHAPTER 3

Throughout that long night, Jonas had not even thought about his flock. He was humbled when he learned that one of his friends who ran the stable on the edge of town had joined Ezekiel on the hill. Abram had been a good friend since childhood, joining Jonas at Hebrew school in their studies of the sacred scrolls many years ago. Abram's stable was regularly used by the few dairy cows in the town, as well as the oxen and donkeys owned by the farmers who needed them for plowing the tough, dry dirt of Judea. Jonas had been to the stable many times, not to shelter his sheep but to greet his good friend once a month or so. For Abram to leave his business to help Jonas during this time of dire need was quite a sacrifice, surmised Jonas. The reality was that Abram wanted to help but could not talk to his friend Jonas without either of them crying so he felt this service more palatable.

Jonas went into the house when the first light appeared over the hill on the eastern horizon. As he entered, he said a prayer that the sickness had passed and Sarah was waking like she normally did. He was nauseated when he saw Esther and three of the other women quietly sobbing around Sarah's bed, watching Sarah's breathing become shallower and clearly labored. He gently picked up Sarah's hand, expecting to feel the fever that had afflicted her but was shaken when he felt her hand cool to the touch. The doctor then told him the fever had broken in the middle of the night but Sarah failed to respond to any methods of stimulation. The doctor lowered his eyes and told Jonas and Esther that Sarah was dying and only God could save her now.

The news hit Jonas like a boulder crushing his chest. He did not notice that Esther was now holding his hand as all he could hear or feel was that Sarah was dying! Esther squeezed his hand hard and led him over to the small bench by the bed in which Sarah lay. One of the ladies who had spent the night here with Esther brought Jonas a small bowl of mutton stew that another of the ladies had brought over last evening.

She begged Jonas, "You haven't eaten a thing all day since returning from the hill yesterday morning."

In reality, Jonas had not eaten anything since dinner the night before, but that did not matter to him.

"You will need your strength to go on. Please eat this."

But Jonas had no appetite and felt nauseous at the thought of food. All he could think of was holding Sarah one last time, holding her till her last breath on this earth carried her into the hands of the Lord.

"I will hold Sarah here. Please help me lift her onto my lap," Jonas said.

Esther and Naomi, crying silently, helped Jonas cradle Sarah's head in his thick arms as her legs lay across his legs, limp and lifeless. Sarah's breathing was now shallow and erratic, with irregular pauses between each labored breath. The clothes she wore on the mountain with Jonas were now piled in a heap in the corner, soiled during her unconscious state. She was wrapped in a sheet, providing her warmth but also accessibility to the doctor and her caretakers. After what seemed like hours but was only a few minutes, Sarah breathed her last. Jonas clutched her small face to his as his tears flowed through his beard and showered her now colorless cheeks. The wailing of his family and the attentive women behind him could be heard several houses away, but Jonas heard none of it. He prayed to his Lord to take *him* also as he was sure he could not go on without Sarah.

This was the worst day of Jonas's life, and he wished it would be his last!

CHAPTER 4

According to Jewish law, Sarah had to be buried within one day, a time frame that Jonas could not accept. Less than thirty-six hours ago, Sarah was racing up the hill to spend the evening with her daddy, and now she was being prepared for burial, the final farewell to the most important person in his life. He thought of the emerging school of thought that death was not the end but the beginning of eternity. Some of his Jewish brethren were even preaching about a resurrection of the body, but this was completely foreign to his Jewish heritage. He choked up in his throat a bit and hoped that he would see her again after this life was over. Again, he hoped that was soon, as the pain was overwhelming him.

Knowing this would be a long day, Jonas tried to eat some brown bread but could not swallow. He pushed it away and went outside. Esther, Naomi, Beth, and three women of the town had spent the past few hours washing Sarah's cold body, wrapping her in a small burial cloth, and carrying her to the burial ground where a small dirt tomb awaited her. Jonas, even with the help of their generous but poor friends, could not afford a tomb hewn from the rock, so a simple burial was required. Jonas wanted to carry her up the hill where she could rest with him forever every night, but this was not permitted by the religious leaders who seemed to have a rule about everything.

After the burial, friends came back to the home where neighboring women had brought a large spread of savory dishes, nourishment for the family and friends who had worked and fretted so much over the past day that personal needs such as food were ignored. While most of the family was observing the Law of sitting shiva, Jonas was unable to embrace this tradition. Ezekiel was there after spending a complete day and night on the hill with the sheep but would return within hours to tend the flock. While his faith dictated this period of mourning, Jonas knew he had to get away as soon as he could for both practical and emotional reasons. The sheep needed tending, and Jonas needed reflective time alone. While Jonas mingled among the neighbors and friends, feigning appreciation that his heart was incapable of at this time, several of the women came forward with misguided attempts at consolation.

"Jonas, you must be strong as your family depends upon you," whispered one elderly woman from whom greater wisdom was expected by Jonas.

Jonas gritted his teeth to prevent an inappropriate response that would cost his wife a valued friendship. Jonas did not want to be *strong*. Jonas wanted to be *dead*!

Another woman approached Jonas and spoke openly, "At least you still have three healthy children at home."

Jonas fought every urge to leave this house right then as he couldn't believe anyone could be so dismissive of his young jewel. He grunted, apparently some form of "thank you" and turned away. It was not as if the love he had for Sarah could be redistributed among the remaining three. Jonas now understood that when a new child is born, love is *multiplied*. But when a child is lost, that same love could not be *redivided*.

Their little town was peaceful by most standards, but the simplest activity annoyed Jonas. The rest of the world seemed to be moving on, with women hauling water and preparing meals, men working the fields and orchards, and children playing as if nothing happened. The only difference was the seclusion that enveloped Jonas, and not knowing whether he was avoiding his friends or whether his friends were avoiding him. The outcome was the same. The hill would be perfect for this much-welcomed quiet seclusion.

Jonas whispered to Esther that he needed to get away for a little bit but he would be back by sundown. Instead of ascending the hill, Jonah walked across town and up the well-worn steps of the town synagogue, a building that pre-dated King David and his family hundreds of years ago. While their town had been invaded and overrun by the Babylonians centuries ago, the building was undamaged, and the sacred scrolls were returned when the Jews returned from captivity. He needed some time to reflect before he spent time with the sheep up on the hill.

Upon entering the old synagogue, Jonas took a seat in the back against the Eastern wall just as the rabbi read from the scrolls a dreary passage from Job.

"*The Lord gave and the Lord has taken away, Blessed be the name of the Lord . . .*"

The reading of the scroll continued but, Jonas heard none of it. Maybe Job could continue to praise the Lord after he lost everything, but Jonas struggled trying to understand his God who had taken *his everything*. The rabbi continued to read from this passage, a passage he had selected to console the people of the town. Everyone knew what had happened to little Sarah, and even those who did not know Jonas and his family grieved at this loss of one of their innocents. And while the rabbi droned on from the scrolls, Jonas heard none of it.

CHAPTER 5

When Jonas returned home from the synagogue, Beth and Naomi hugged their father longer than normal, knowing how much he hurt. They had spent the morning with their mother and the ladies of the town preparing Sarah's little body for the burial. They had cried most of the morning, preparing the spices to be used in the ritual burial, as the Law dictated a natural burial with no embalming or cremation. They accompanied their parents and the townspeople to the grave site, joining the chorus of muffled sobs from their neighbors and friends.

Even though they knew he should be sitting shiva with the rest of the family, the girls had packed a dinner for their daddy to take up the mountain, with some of the sweets that the neighbors had brought after the burial. Each of them wrote a short note they secreted into his pack to take for a night with the flock. Naomi asked if he would like her to accompany him tonight, but Jonas quickly declined, insisting that she stay with her mother. Without giving her any other reasons for this decision, the reality is that he wanted time by himself and he couldn't bear the thought of another of his girls getting sick.

In actuality, his thoughts were not of his girls "getting sick" but self-centered on "Jonas getting another of his daughters sick." The guilt that weighed upon his heart was unbearable. His father had taught him since he was a young boy that it was a father's responsibility to provide for his family and protect his family. In his mind, he was a failure, either for exposing Sarah to her fatal sickness or for failing to protect her when she needed him most. The outcome was the same. Jonas had lost his daughter, his trust in God, and his will to live, all within a bitter three-day period.

Naomi, sensing the cloud of depression overwhelming her Father, again asked Jonas if she could join him tonight.

"NO!" His answer was as terse and thunderous as any in the family had ever heard.

Both girls and Esther recoiled, withdrawing a short distance away from Jonas, sensing quite correctly that any interaction with him at this time was not in their best interest. When Esther tried to soothe Jonas with consoling words, Jonas wanted nor tolerated any of it. He grabbed his backpack, exited without another word, and headed up the hill to tend the flock.

When he reached the site of the nightly campfire, he met Ezekiel as he packed his goods for his descent down the hill and a night at home. Caesar was lying by the site of the fire, lacking his typical energy level, almost detecting that Sarah had not been here for the past two nights.

As Ezekiel came to greet his Father with a kiss, Jonas snapped, "Why is this dog lying here? Look at those sheep wandering down the hill. What have you two been doing when you were supposed to be working?"

The boy had never heard his father speak to him in such irascible tones at any time in his life! Without giving his father the traditional kiss, Ezekiel gathered his things and left without uttering a word.

Just moments later, after his son was out of earshot, Jonas regretted both the message and tone with which he verbally assaulted Ezekiel. While he would apologize later when he saw his son, he knew that he had inflicted a wound that would never completely heal. Caesar kept his distance as well, sensing correctly that Jonas wanted to be alone. The dog went back to the flock and herded two strays that had wandered a dangerous distance from the flock and then settled down near the sheep, away from his usually attentive master. Caesar could not understand what was wrong, but he clearly sensed that something was wrong.

Now Jonas realized that he had forgotten the kindling that would provide light and warmth on the brisk night. He did not care that he might catch a cold on a night like this as that could only hasten his desired exit from this miserable existence. He considered collecting dung from the animals to burn, but that required an energy that currently eluded him. As he unrolled the pack he grabbed in haste, he saw the lambskin and flute that one of the girls had packed with his dinner. He wasn't sure if this was packed by habit or intentionally inserted in an errant attempt to provide some measure of comfort. This unexpected reminder of Sarah choked Jonas briefly, and he contemplated using this as fuel for tonight's scant fire. When he untied the leather straps, however, and saw the flute he had meticulously crafted for Sarah, Jonas was overcome by a stabbing in his chest he had not anticipated. He looked heavenward into the clear, dark winter sky, fingered the holes of the tiny flute, and rubbed the lambskin across his rough face, trying to smell any memory of Sarah. Tears silently rolled down his cheeks, and he decided he could never part with Sarah's valued keepsakes.

Jonas wandered the top third of the hill looking for anything that he might burn when he came across the small patch of poppies, now near their wintery sleep, that Sarah had planted for him. Jonas dropped all he had collected, fell to his knees, and wept loudly.

"HOW COULD YOU TAKE HER AND LEAVE ME!" Jonas shouted to the God he had trusted and loved. "WHY HER?"

Mucus ran from his nose freely, filling his beard with a disgusting flow that threatened to freeze. He didn't care as it didn't matter. Nothing mattered. Nothing mattered at all.

CHAPTER 6

Three years had now passed since Sarah died. Esther had spent a great deal of time with her friends at the well, some of whom has lost children during their earlier years or at childbirth. She had come to accept that Sarah was gone and she had responsibilities and obligations to care for Naomi, Beth, Ezekiel, and hardest of all, Jonas. Jonas no longer listened to the family at meals or engaged in the discussions, eating very small portions of most dinners and quickly leaving for the hill and his personal self-imposed prison of solitude. Esther prayed for her husband, hoping he would find peace and healing. She missed the times of intimacy they had enjoyed for so many years prior to Sarah's death. The few times they had relations since then were perfunctory and unfulfilling, leaving both of them frustrated and remorseful.

Jonas was leaving for the hill earlier and staying later, hoping in vain that the extended distraction of his work hours would dull the ever-present pain. It did provide him with time alone, time when he was not barking at his family in staccato directives that made them feel like hired staff and not members of the family. Jonas had seen his friend Abram, the stable keeper, only four times during these three years. Neither man was comfortable discussing Sarah or feelings or anything that would open the floodgate of emotions that both of them desperately wanted to avoid with the other. Abram had helped Jonas drive some of the flock to Jerusalem the past two years, while Ezekiel tended the remaining sheep on the hill. The trips were uneventful, with Jonas leading the flock as the shepherd recognized by the sheep and Abram serving as a sweeper to ensure stragglers were included throughout the course of the journey. This arrangement provided a sense of partnership and support without requiring uncomfortable conversation. Both men knew they were friends, but neither wanted to broach this topic of discussion, and neither did so.

This past trip to Jerusalem had been exceptionally difficult as Caesar Augustus had ordered a census of his entire empire, clearly an effort to increase the taxes paid to the emperor they all loathed. The road to Jerusalem, normally lightly travelled this time of year, was congested by travelers on mandated sojourns to their hometowns to meet the dictates of the emperor. This made driving the flock down the road exceptionally difficult, weaving the flock among families on foot, broken wagons, and a myriad of travelers moving against the flow of the majority. His little town was filled with families travelling to the hometown of their family origins. As Jonas's family had settled here since the Jews left Babylon more than twenty generations ago, he was not required to endure the hardships of travel so many of these poor families had to shoulder. He merely completed the census requirements by reporting to the local authorities. He cynically awaited the inevitable outcome of increased taxes that would further stress his ability to support his family and accentuate his feeling of familial inadequacy.

Tonight was the coldest he could remember in the past several years. A cloudless sky with adequate lighting from the half moon, Jonas huddled near the fire with Caesar curled up at his feet. As he had done every night for the past three years, Jonas untied the leather straps on the sheepskin and took out the wooden flute that Sarah had played do adeptly. He no longer cried every time he opened it except for those nights of her birthday, holidays, and the anniversary of her death. On those nights, the stabbing in his chest was as painful as ever, but the duration between these stabbings grew longer.

Esther also mourned these days when family was most treasured and their children respected their grieving but no longer mourned openly. They used the days to recollect the joyous memories of their baby sister, remembering the songs she played, the games she enjoyed, and the tricks she had taught Caesar, now aged and slowing. They could still bribe Caesar into doing his old tricks with small pieces of dried meat, but he did not perform with the same energy as when prompted by Sarah.

By now, Jonas had lost quite a bit of his body weight, failing to eat properly for the past three years. He had begun to pack an old wineskin with cheap wine each evening, telling himself it helped him sleep and keep warm on nights just such as this. In reality, it dulled the pain and distracted him from the loneliness he now regretted but could not erase. As it had been three years, everyone assumed he had recovered from his loss and resumed his lifestyle. Only Esther knew the truth that her warm, loving husband Jonas had been replaced by a bitter, angry man who ate too little and drank too much. Jonas pulled the stopper from the wineskin, lifted the opening to his lips, and took two greedy swallows of the cheap wine. As he wiped the remnants from his now unkempt beard, Jonas looked down the hill toward the outskirts of his small town and rubbed his aging eyes in an attempt to clarify what he was seeing.

CHAPTER 7

As he rubbed the campfire smoke from his eyes, he looked down the hill and was amazed by the caravan below him. Camels! With riders! These were not Jewish visitors answering the call of the emperor's census, as their clothes were foreign from the kingdoms far to the East. And while he had seen these massive dromedaries once before when he was a much younger man, camels were rarely seen in this small town well removed from the busy trade routes of Jerusalem. They were dismounting and unpacking items at Abram's livestock cave near the edge of the town, a curious destination for men of such lofty status! He had to see what was happening and why was it happening *here* of all places.

Caesar wanted to follow his master down the hill but dutifully obeyed when Jonas ordered him to tend to the sheep. To discourage any curious animals from exploring his pack looking for food, Jonas threw the satchel over his shoulder, took his staff to ensure stability walking the rocky path down the hill in the dark, and began the walk to Abram's place. He stopped, realizing he had not eaten nor fed Caesar, and threw the entire portion of dried mutton from his pack to the dog. Besides, he had little appetite for food. He brought the wineskin with him more for thirst than personal enjoyment. The bitter cold evening air chilled his lungs, and his breath was even more visible as his paced quickened down toward the stable.

Upon arrival, he met Abram just outside the cave, also enthralled with the tall beasts of burden that would not even fit through the low-hanging top of the cave, converted to a stable several generations ago.

"Hello, Jonas. It is so good to see you, but I am surprised it is tonight," Abram stated as he embraced his childhood friend.

"It is not every day that we see camels in this part of the country and ridden by such men of obvious wealth," Jonas replied. "What brought them to our village and why would they ever stop at your stable?"

With a piece of straw hanging from his near toothless mouth, Abram explained how they were astrologers and were exploring a new star that foretold the birth of a king. That still didn't explain to either of these men why they sought this newborn king in Abram's stable but neither pursued that line of questioning as Abram was thankful for the fee to feed the camels, and Jonas frankly didn't care about their silly search. Royalty in this stable? Right.

As Jonas entered the cave, he saw a young mother, no more than sixteen years of age, who had recently given birth to her first son. Standing with them and trying in vain to shield them from the cold wind blowing through the opening of the stable, a young man with thick, muscular arms tried to comfort his new wife and son. They were poor, badly underdressed for both the cold weather and the journey. Abram explained to Jonas that the census had filled all available housing in their town and his stable was available for this shelter. The straw that covered the floor of the stable forbade the building of a fire and the cold within the humble structure was oppressive.

The baby boy had been crying since Jonas arrived, and the intensity of his crying seemed to be increasing. His limbs seemed to be shivering as the young mother tried unsuccessfully to nurse the baby while warming him at her breast. It was then that the first of the foreign visitors stepped forth and, bowing deeply and reverently at the waist, held a small box, ornate with jewels and ivory. The only ivory either Jonas or Abram had ever seen was in the Temple in Jerusalem, a gift to Solomon from the Queen of Sheba. This treasure was successfully hidden during several conquests and had been returned to the Temple sometime long before Jonas and Abram were born. The first of these three visitors was dark skinned with long dark hair, with pieces of golden cloth decorating the ends. His garments were glistening in the light from the hanging lamp, and an unfamiliar fur lined the collar.

The young father opened the box and saw gold coins, more than this young father had ever held in his life. "Your generosity humbles us," the young man whispered in an attempt to sooth his son.

While Jonas and all of his neighbors spoke Hebrew, the young couple surprised him by speaking in Aramaic, a tongue more widely used in the region of Galilee to the north. He understood their language but refrained from showing his limited linguistic skills. The mother, however, was concerned that even this much gold might not save her newborn son from this brutal night. Jonas could not have spoken if he wanted to as this scenario reminded him of his Sarah.

The second visitor stepped forward just a short distance from the feeding trough that the young couple had used as the baby's bed. He knelt before the young father and held the father's hands to his forehead, a form of supplication that was not common in the Jewish culture, but apparently the ritual from one of the eastern lands. One of his servants then handed him a large urn, filled with spicy aromatic powder that Jonas knew to be frankincense. When burned, this expensive luxury would fill the surrounding area with wafts of smoke one could only expect to enjoy in one of Herod's palaces or in the Temple during the High Holy Days. The young couple marveled at the generosity of these foreign visitors but spoke quietly to each other that this was not going to help their newborn son tonight. The mother forced a thankful smile though she realized that the substantial value of this gift was impractical on a cold night like this!

The infant was crying steadily, and a faint shiver could be seen even under his swaddling wrap. As the new mother tried to both feed her son and suppress this crying, the third man stepped forward, carrying a glazed alabaster jug filled with a thick golden oil that the elderly Gentile man announced as myrrh. The man explained that myrrh was used to anoint the bodies of royalty upon their death, a sign of tribute to a man of greatness. The top of the jar was removed, and the fragrance of the oil filled the cold air in the stable that normally reeked of animal dung this time of night. By now, tears streamed silently down the smooth cheeks of the young mother, in sharp contrast to the louder bellowing of her infant son.

"I am grateful that you have travelled so far to honor our son and regret we have very little to offer in hospitality," the young girl lamented.

Jonas and Abram were far enough away that they heard only fragments of the follow on conversation, of what drew these men and their entourages to Abram's stable. They heard a few words about their visit to King Herod and following some new star that rose in the East. Jonas feigned interest in their origins as all he could think about was that there was none of this fancy myrrh offered or available for his Sarah's burial. They had washed her little body, wrapped it in accordance with the Law, and spiced it with the few meager additives they could afford. Now foreign visitors have travelled for many weeks to arrive at Abram's stable with gifts of such value to honor the poor baby boy. Jonas stood in the background, hurt and angry that he could not afford anything like this to anoint his little Sarah and no men of nobility or stature had ventured forth to volunteer their help.

CHAPTER 8

After an abbreviated farewell to the young family, the foreign visitors mounted their camels and lumbered away in the direction opposite of their arrival. Abram told Jonas that they had been warned about the treachery of King Herod and were advised to steer clear of Jerusalem. The politics of Jerusalem was beyond Jonas's concern, so he directed his focus elsewhere. By now, the young mother was praying that God would protect her son. The infant was shaking, and his little voice was faltering as the extended crying in this frigid night had robbed him of his normal level of vocals. The baby's father had removed his tunic and wrapped his teenage bride and son, trying to warm, comfort, and console them, even at the risk of his own health. She sobbed that the baby was shaking and would not even try to feed anymore.

Jonas, fearing for the health of this young boy, now stepped forward and reached into his pack. Choking back the tears that always appeared when he untied the pack, Jonas removed the small flute and handed the thick sheep skin to the young mother. "This was my daughter's blanket and will keep your son warm this night."

He never thought he would part with this treasure, but he could not sit back and watch this young couple experience the pain of loss that he continued to experience.

As soon as the young mother wrapped the child in the warm sheep skin, the boy stopped crying, the shivering stopped, and he fed hungrily from his mother's breast. As Jonas turned to leave the stable, unwilling to show his tears, the young father shouted after him, "Tonight you have saved our son's life. Please thank your daughter for us!"

Abram started after his friend, hoping to offer a consoling word and a warm embrace, but Jonas quickened his pace so as to maintain his misguided dignity. The infant's father was heard uttering a traditional blessing, "Blessed are You, Lord, King of the Universe, who has granted us life, sustained us, and enabled us to reach this occasion."

Jonas slowly climbed the hill back to his flock, the cold night air no longer burning his lungs. As he reached the top of the hill, he was relieved to see the flock and Caesar resting peacefully in the hilltop meadow. The shepherd stirred the embers, added some animal dung and some scarce twigs he had collected ascending the hill, and was pleased when the fire slowly reignited, warming his feet that had ached for the past few hours. Jonas now held Sarah's little flute, and fondly remembered how it used to bring him so much joy.

As he sat near his campfire, he carefully put Sarah's flute to his lips. Jonas clumsily played the song he taught her years before and could now sense the calm that caressed his slumbering flock. Caesar, hearing the familiar flute so long missing on the hill, sauntered over to Jonas and curled up on the warmed feet of his master. Both enjoyed this innocent intimacy long missing between these old friends. Jonas laid back on the ground, a smile crossing the face that had not smiled for years. In spite of his clumsy playing of the flute, it sounded like a chorus of angels to Jonas.

Just as he began to slumber, he noticed a large star he had never before noticed as it seemed to shower Abram's small stable with a brilliant light. The light also illuminated his hill and allowed him to see the purple poppy flowers that were not there when he left the hill earlier that evening. Jonas leaned forward to smell the unseasonal blooms and recoiled with a pleasant memory.

That is the fragrance I remember from Sarah's blanket. I just never recognized it before, Jonas thought to himself. Her blanket was gone, but God had provided a reminder of Sarah's floral bouquet.

The wind, once bitterly cold, now seemed to sing a heavenly song that warmed Jonas on this cold night. With Caesar curled up at his feet, Jonas quietly whispered good night to Sarah as drifted off to peaceful rest.

CHAPTER 9

As the orange and yellow light of the morning appeared on the eastern horizon, Jonas packed his bedroll and awaited the arrival of Ezekiel. Caesar also awaited the younger man as he would be bringing breakfast for the dog. When Ezekiel's head crested the summit, Caesar ran to meet him with an apparent loyalty that was more likely induced by morning hunger. Jonas walked toward his son and, without uttering a word, hugged his oldest child in an embrace that was longer than usual. Both men knew this was an apology by Jonas for the many harsh words uttered to Ezekiel over the past few years. A tear ran down Jonas's cheek, a tear that was sensed but unseen by his son, and Jonas knew that everything was going to be better. While Jonas's son knew nothing about the poor family in the stable and the exotic visitors last night, Ezekiel could sense a dramatic change in his father's demeanor. It was unusual for Jonas to linger about the mountaintop after being relieved by his son, but Ezekiel welcomed the added attention and affection from his father.

Finally ready to head for home, Jonas again hugged his son, patted Caesar behind his left ear, and began the descent down the rocky path. He wondered how the young couple and their baby were this morning, but he was anxious to get home to see his girls. Upon entering the house, he smelled bread baking and saw a variety of cheeses and dried herring on the rough wooden table he had inherited when his father passed. Naomi and Beth were surprised to see their father with a renewed energy and enthusiastically offered him the mint tea that was available every morning in their home. Jonas thanked them, said a prayer of thanks, completed his ritual washing, and hungrily attacked the breakfast offerings.

"Where is your mother?" Jonas asked, knowing full well that she had gone to the well with the other women.

Naomi answered, "She has gone for water, but she should be back any minute."

As she said this, Esther walked through the door carrying the daily water jug, surprised to see her husband eating breakfast so voraciously.

"I pray you had a peaceful night up top," Esther spoke gingerly, concerned with his unpredictable temper and not yet aware of Jonas's newfound peace and joy.

"I had an amazing night!" exclaimed Jonas, who went on to detail the young family with the newborn baby boy in Abram's stable, the wealthy Gentile visitors with their expensive gifts, and the camels! His daughters had only heard of camels and wanted to run to Abram's to see these pack animals, but Jonas explained how their visit was short and these rich men had left for home in the middle of the night. Jonas suggested that the whole family pack some food to take to the stable for the family and wondered aloud whether they could host this family within their small home until they were able to travel home. Naomi and Beth loved babies and made the de facto decision without input from their mother. With that, the decision was final, and they packed a freshly baked loaf of bread, a sumptuous assortment of cheeses, and the dried herring left over from Jonas's morning feast.

The girls, carrying the breakfast to the stable, ran ahead of their parents, anxious to see the baby. When they arrived at the opening of the dingy cave, Abram met them and explained that the young couple had left already. Jonas and Esther were arriving when Abram explained that when he got to the stable before sunrise, a young man in a white robe was reclining there. The young man told Abram that the couple had packed and fled without notice toward the south. For a reason that was not explained to Abram, they were travelling to Egypt, even though he had learned they were from Nazareth. They all wondered whether they would return to Nazareth eventually and whether those travels would bring them back through their town of Bethlehem.

Jonas entered the stable, reflecting upon the wonderful evening he had spent here just a few hours earlier. Laying across the manger in which the baby slept, he spotted a lambskin much like the one he had given to the baby last night. Unlike Sarah's lambskin, however, this one was a brilliant white, brighter than any wool skin he had ever seen. Jonas picked up the skin, rubbed it across his ruddy face, and was surprised that it was warm, inexplicable on this cool morning. He held the blanket to his cheek, closed his eyes, and smiled. He smelled that heavenly fragrance that he knew to be from Sarah!

From that moment on, Jonas knew that his Sarah was with the Lord and that he would see her again. He gently grasped Esther's hand, pulled her close, and said, "Let's go home."

ABOUT THE AUTHOR

Raised and educated in Cincinnati, Ohio, John Raterman has lived with his wife of more than forty years in the Atlanta area. Throughout these forty years, John and Mary have lost three children to a rare mitochondrial disease and two other daughters have been profoundly affected by this malady. John has retired from his career as an executive with a capital equipment company and holds thirty patents through the company.

For the past twenty years, John and Mary have fostered more than 125 newborn children awaiting adoption by fine Christian families through The Open Door Agency out of Thomasville, Georgia. They are pleased to have families all over the United States and Canada with whom they have fostered children.